YO
COMPLETE
SCORPIO 2023
PERSONAL
HOROSCOPE

Monthly Astrological Prediction Forecast
Readings of Every Zodiac Astrology Sun Star
Signs- Love, Romance, Money, Finances, Career,
Health, Travel, Spirituality.

Iris Quinn

Alpha Zuriel Publishing

Your Complete Scorpio 2023 Personal Horoscope/ Iris Quinn.
-- 1st ed.

We are born at a specific time and place, and, like vintage years of wine, we have the characteristics of the year and season in which we are born. Astrology claims nothing more.
— CARL JUNG

CONTENTS

CHAPTER ONE

SCORPIO

Constellation: Scorpio

Zodiac symbol: Scorpion

Date: October 22 – November 21

Zodiac element: Water

Zodiac quality: Fixed

Greatest Compatibility: Cancer and Taurus

Sign ruler: Mars, Pluto

Day: Tuesday

Color: Red

Birthstone: Topaz

SCORPIO TRAITS

- The primary feeling is betrayal.
- Okay with awkward silence.
- I'm not sure whether they're serious or joking.
- Eyes that gaze deep into your soul.

PERSONALITY OF SCORPIO

Scorpio personality is a vast gulf of endless complexities (or at least how they project themselves). They are difficult to understand. They function as psychological trap doors.

They socialize through a double-sided mirror, constantly scanning and reading you while you can only see your own reflection. They would rather be the ones asking the questions. They use their perceptive scalpel to remove your skin and inventory your throbbing viscera. They prod and prod. They are aware of the minor details that make you tick. Your stress spots. The deceptive methods they use to obtain the answer they desire. They are acutely aware of power, its flows, and their place within it.

Scorpios, despite their propensity to be widely popular, have a highly lonely nature. They have a brutal outlook on life. Either eat or be eaten. Every human encounter involves the clash of opposing tremendous forces. A confrontation of wants and needs in which someone wins and someone loses. Their understanding of other people's interior systems offers them an advantage over their competitors. They understand how to pit people against each other. They can be forthcoming and elusive at the same time, depending on the situation. They are direct, but not without tact. They are deliberate in the information they reveal. They're not liars, and they don't spread lies, but they're masters at revealing some truths while hiding others behind heavy curtains.

WEAKNESSES OF SCORPIO

Scorpios are not terrified of most things that other people are afraid of. Not at all. Not suffering. Not even death. They face these realities head on. They understand that death is unavoidable. Instead of inciting terror, this information sharpens their enthusiasm for life. Scorpios live on the precipice of the unknown. That makes life more fascinating.

Scorpios are afraid of being exposed. The sensation of being recognized. Darkness can be a safe haven. Pain can be used to justify not trusting. When they open themselves, they give others authority over them, and Scorpios require control. In the face of an otherwise unpredictable environment, the illusion of control over themselves and others is the only thing that makes them feel secure.

RELATIONSHIP COMPATIBILITY WITH SCORPIO

Based only on their Sun signs, this is how Scorpio interacts with others. These are the compatibility interpretations for all 12 potential Scorpio combinations. This is a limited and insufficient method of determining compatibility.

However, Sun-sign compatibility remains the foundation for overall harmony in a relationship.

The general rule is that yin and yang do not get along. Yin complements yin, and yang complements yang. While yin and yang partnerships can be successful, they require more effort. Earth and water zodiac signs are both Yin. Yang is represented by the fire and air zodiac signs.

Aries and Scorpio

A partnership between Scorpio and Aries will quickly become difficult. Physical intimacy is the best common ground for these two to understand each other. They are, nonetheless, profoundly different in their ways of thinking and feeling. Scorpio desires complete control over the relationship and its partner, but Aries is unwilling to give it up. They are best suited to an occasional relationship.

Taurus and Scorpio

When Scorpio and Taurus join forces, the passion, sensuality, and eroticism will be spectacular. However, certain occurrences in ordinary life can generate speed bumps in this relationship. Scorpio is far too domineering. Taurus will not be able to withstand the emotional stings that Scorpio will undoubtedly deliver. Scorpio must accept Taurus as they are for this partnership to work.

Gemini and Scorpio

If Scorpio and Gemini meet together just for the purpose of mutual intimate pleasure, it can be a lovely experience for both of you. However, if you want to progress and create a relationship, you will have to walk a hard route together if you want it to succeed. Scorpio's jealousy and eruptions will destroy Gemini's chances of remaining by its side.

Cancer and Scorpio

Scorpio and Cancer relationships can be quite gratifying if Cancer is willing to let Scorpio take the lead. Cancer should not be concerned about its safety because Scorpio will provide them with whatever they require. In turn, Cancer will shower Scorpio with boundless affection and pleasure. Scorpio is less aggressive than usual in such a partnership.

Leo and Scorpio

Scorpio and Leo have an extremely tough time staying together in a love partnership. They may be fine for the odd connection, but they are not so good for long-term stability. To complement Scorpio, Leo must set aside its most prominent characteristics: forceful voice, decisiveness, independence, and control. Scorpio will never tolerate such traits in its companion.

Virgo and Scorpio

Scorpio and Virgo might have a really excellent partnership. Scorpio will be pleased with its adored Virgo since Virgo will appreciate Scorpio's accomplishments and will not be as critical as other signs. Scorpio's temper tantrums and feelings of jealousy will be handled well by Virgo, who has great analytical skills.

Libra and Scorpio

Scorpio and Libra relationships can be happy and stable. Scorpio must control its possessive and jealous outbursts. Scorpio can give Libra a sense of safety that Libra doesn't have because Libra is always questioning things and trying to find a better balance.

Scorpio and Scorpio

To maintain a stable relationship, two Scorpios must put in the effort on a daily basis. Scorpios are fiery, jealous, and domineering. They should learn to regulate those traits so that their relationship does not suffer. On a bodily level, both Scorpios will understand each other completely. They will keep their passionate but volatile romance going.

Sagittarius and Scorpio

Scorpio and Sagittarius will initially enjoy their partnership to the fullest: adventures, sensuality, passion, and pleasure. But if Scorpio and Sagittarius want to live together, they will have to work together to solve the problems that have come up because of their major clash: Scorpio's possessiveness and jealousy will clash with Sagittarius' desire for independence and growth.

Capricorn and Scorpio

Scorpio and Capricorn might be a good fit. Scorpio's intuition combines with Capricorn's depth of analysis, and they will have many wonderful times learning new things about themselves and the world around them. They should be careful not to separate themselves from the rest of the world too much.

Aquarius and Scorpio

A partnership between Scorpio and Aquarius is conceivable, but it will require a great deal of tolerance on both sides. Scorpio is too rigid and regimented to grasp Aquarius' yearning for freedom and movement. Aquarius will close down or decide to leave the partnership if Scorpio does not lessen its demands.

Pisces and Scorpio

Scorpio and Pisces have a great partnership because they both feel understood and emotionally contained. Both Pisces and Scorpio prioritize the emotional and spiritual sides of life, and they understand each other brilliantly in this regard. Scorpio's explosive instincts will be tempered by Pisces' tenderness.

LOVE AND PASSION

A fulfilling love life is quite important to most Scorpios. They must express their most private feelings. Their strong sexual appeal makes it quite easy for them to locate mates.

When they choose someone, they want complete dedication, they refuse to accept "no" for an answer, and when they are rejected, they reveal their most obsessive side.

Making love is Scorpio's deepest form of expression and a crucial component in all relationships. They have a lot of fun with their partner and have a busy social life, but without proper sexual commitment, the relationship is doomed to fail.

They make excellent lovers, frequently removing their partner's inhibitions.

Those around them, on the other hand, must have high psychological resistance to offset their constant mood fluctuations. Those who do well will gain a wealth of experience that few others can match.

MARRIAGE

Scorpios have a difficult time finding love. They want to experience everything and are accustomed to having multiple relationships at the same time. They are unlikely to be unfaithful once married. They become devoted and loving lovers who are always willing to help their mate.

When they are insecure, they experience envy and need time to reestablish trust in the other person.

They are not afraid to put all of their financial, physical, and emotional resources at the disposal of their partner and strive hard to keep their partnership together. The ties they form become increasingly strong over time.

Scorpio wives are ambitious and intellectual, with the energy to balance their family and work responsibilities.

Scorpio men are powerful and devoted, although sometimes they go through long periods of silence.

CHAPTER TWO

SCORPIO 2023 HOROSCOPE

Overview Scorpio 2023

In 2023, Jupiter will transit the 6th house of Aries until May, following which it will transit the 7th house of Taurus. This would cause several financial issues in the year's first quarter. However, its transit to the 7th house will bring excellent fortune to Scorpios in love or marriage. Saturn, the planet of discipline, will be transiting the 4th house of Aquarius until March when it will change to the 5th house of Pisces.

When Saturn transits Aquarius, it impacts your domestic life and well-being. Its transit through Pisces has an impact on your love life as well as your relationships with children if you have any.

Regarding the outer planets, Uranus is transiting into Scorpio's 7th house of Taurus, which governs their relationships. Neptune enters the 5th house of Pisces, while Pluto transits the 3rd house of Capricorn until May/June 2023, when it switches to the 4th house of Aquarius.

With this yearly transit, both the outer and inner planets have the potential to interfere with Scorpios' lives.

Scorpios' love and marriage prospects will benefit from a serene atmosphere in 2023, thanks to Venus, the planet of love. Venus' transit through the zodiac sky will be beneficial to your love life. Things can also become complex at times. It is recommended that Scorpios form long-lasting ties. Accept individuals as they come into your life, let go of your ego, and love and affectionately hug your partner/spouse throughout the year.

Scorpios' professional and business chances would be excellent in 2023. Natives will benefit from services as the year begins. However, if you want long-term rewards, you must put in a lot of effort and dedication. Saturn's transit after the first quarter of the year would result in beneficial improvements in your job field. If you desire to establish your own business, there is plenty of opportunities. In this regard, do not disregard the advice of elders and peers. Scorpios interested in business will find that partnerships yield wonderful results. Workplace problems do arise from time to time. There may be occasions when you have an incompatible relationship with a coworker.

Scorpios could expect to be happy and healthy in the coming year. Since Jupiter is in the 8th house and Saturn is in the 10th house in relation to your Ascendant house, you should be fine. You would have a lot of energy, and your immune system would be strong for the time of year.

Scorpios' financial situation will improve this year. This would be a profitable era since Jupiter would be aspecting your 11th house of profits. The inflow of wealth would be continuous and would not stop. However, Scorpios are encouraged to limit their spending, which might strain their budgets. They are urged to avoid speculative dealings, gambling, and high-value purchases for the remainder of the year. This cannot be avoided when it comes to medical expenses for family members. Make a plan for the worst-case scenario.

For the Scorpios, the year 2023 begins with a hint of great sadness regarding family. Saturn being in your 4th house of home life and happiness means that there will be a lot of problems and delays. If someone in your family died or got sick, it would weigh you down. Things will improve when it moves into the fifth house of Pisces in March. Family members would notice your actions, and your goals for home life would slowly start to take shape.

Scorpios will have an average year in terms of travel this year. Jupiter's aspect on the 9th house promises long-distance travel for the locals this year. They are also likely to travel abroad due to the Moon's node's aspect on the 12th house. Natives are more inclined to go to distant regions for study, work, or pilgrimage. This year, some Scorpios will be able to return home after a long absence.

Scorpio people interested in spiritual things will have a good year in 2023. You could worship your native god and become more spiritual. Ask for the blessings of older people and religious leaders because you can learn from them and follow their advice during this time. Donate to charity and do social work that will make you feel good about yourself.

Scorpios should try to keep their distance this year, which will help ease tensions. A good year is promised, but Scorpios are told not to be in a hurry and to take things slowly. You would benefit from being patient and persistent in the coming year. Don't be too emotional with your partner, and don't keep anything from them.

January 2023

Horoscope

Capricorn's energies limit your options, which is in your best interest. The Aquarius planets are eager to provoke you, but if you play the game, you may escape their annoying consequences. You may not be swamped with invitations and trips if you focus on the planets in pleasant signs. What you can expect: a routine existence with no shocks. As an alternative, it ensures your complete tranquilly from every angle.

Be prepared for an uncomfortable journey if you venture outside your comfort zone. When it comes to Aquarius, you're in for a treat that's both intriguing and conflictual at the same time.

Love

Your best friend isn't Venus. His being in Aquarius means there will be annoyances, misunderstandings, and other roadblocks. What looks simple is hard to do after the fourth. As of the 28th, when Venus move into Pisces, calm and harmony returns to your life.

Uranus makes the annoying effects of the planets in Aquarius even worse. If you want peace, stay away from the devil. If, despite your best efforts, your partner goes crazy, just wait. On the 28th, everything is in order because Venus is in Pisces.

Single Scorpio, Use the energies of Mercury in Capricorn to avoid being let down. Take the chance to strengthen relationships, and don't get too lazy in case of an unexpected encounter. Be wise enough to wait until the end of the month if you want to get further.

Career

There will be times when you feel overwhelmed by how much is going on. You'll also have times when things are quiet that will worry you. Scorpio, don't think that other people are trying to hurt you. Jupiter is in sector six of your solar chart, and he is the one who makes your career go up and down. So when you have a lot of work to do, don't count the hours, and when things slow down, take a break.

The way the stars are aligned this month doesn't give you much hope for your career. You would be obsessed with how uncertain you feel about your job. This would change how you run your business or do your job.

It's possible that you could work very hard to reach your goals but still not reach them. You would change jobs or make significant changes to how your business works. But none of this would make you happy. There is also the chance of getting into a big fight with your boss or business partner. This should be avoided as much as possible. Try to think ahead and take care of problems before they get worse.

Finance

On the money side, it's the same battle! Slow down on your spending so that your money doesn't run out at the wrong time.

From what the stars say, it looks like this month won't be good for your finances. There is a good chance that your relationship with your bosses would get so bad that you would lose their trust, especially if you see that serious losses are coming. You should be able to avoid this by being prepared and thinking ahead.

Taking business risks would also likely cause some of you to lose a lot of money. So, you shouldn't take part in any kind of gambling. Also, the climate would not be very good for investments or starting new businesses. So, for now, you should put such opportunities on hold.

Health

This month, no favorable collection of circumstances will encourage your excellent health, as the stars are not in a supportive mood. Any tendency to chronic conditions such as rheumatism, gas, and excess wind in the digestive tract would irritate you more than usual. As a result, more care would be required.

Investigate any chronic cough very carefully, as this might be an indication of a rheumatic heart at the moment. There should be no negligence on this score; take adequate precautions. This month, you should also prioritize your dental health. This month, pay extra attention to your teeth since they may be bothering you.

Travel

A great month to make significant gains from travel since the omens from the stars are auspicious. You would most likely travel alone by rail or road, with some air travel thrown in for good measure. A journey overseas is also not out of the question.

You would be highly successful in your journeys since not all of your trips would be linked to your career or business. Travel will expose you to new people and open up new doors of opportunity. The most promising direction would be East.

Insight from the stars

You can cross the boundary if you believe your universe is too tiny. This is possible, but only if you remain calm under all conditions. This month, you must be patient with yourself. You've done your part, and now you must wait patiently for the universe to do its own.

February 2023

Horoscope

The energies that come from Pisces make your field of action more extensive. They make you feel at ease, which brings out the best in you. They understand how you feel and what you want to do. The weeks of routine and being alone are coming to an end.

This month, good things are going to happen. You will still have to deal with the conflicting energies that come from Aquarius, though. They cause misunderstandings in your relationship, which can make you act in extreme ways that don't show who you are. Around the 5th, this effect gets stronger when the Full Moon is in Leo. If you want to keep the peace, don't cross the border of your universe and test the devil.

Love

The energies from Capricorn and Pisces help improve the area of your life you love. But watch out for Uranus in Taurus, which tries to push you into your comfort zones. Don't take everything at face value to avoid these problems.

Scorpio, your peaceful way of life is favored. On the other hand, with your partner, things can get stuck. This month, you should get a list of complaints that you should answer calmly.

Single Scorpio, Planets in friendly signs work together to bring you together with someone who has everything you need to be happy. If you want the magic to work, don't always say you're on your own.

Career

Even though this area is doing pretty well, you might not be happy with it. Around the 5th, you might feel like your progress is being slowed down or that you are in a bad environment. Scorpio, get rid of your bad thoughts because they'll make you make a wrong choice. Instead, try to see the good things about yourself and the people around you. If you do this, you'll find that everything is fine.

This month, it looks like your career will move forward in a good way. There is a good chance that you could make a lot of progress in your career if you worked with several intelligent people. You would also get a lot from your bosses, even though you might have serious disagreements with some of them.

There would also be a lot of moving around. All of this would be pretty helpful. In fact, there is a good chance that you will get a new job or make significant changes to how your business operates, which will necessitate your relocation. There is a good chance that your efforts will help you reach the goals you set.

Finance

On the money side, things are stable as far as the money you need to live each day. On the other hand, if you want to invest, ignore what other people say.

Based on what the stars say, your financial future will be promising this month. Writers, poets, and other artists like them would do well at what they do and be known for it.

You will get enough money to take care of yourself and your family. Taking care of your money with discipline will help you pay for your family's daily needs.

Things point to the fact that you would make money from the investments you make. Many people will advise you on how to make more money, but you have to be very careful to get rid of the ones that don't fit your goals and values.

Health

This month, the stars in front of you are good for your health. People with sensitive chests or lungs prone to health problems in these areas are likely to feel a lot better. There is a chance that overworking yourself will make you tired and weak.

You could easily avoid this if you didn't push yourself too hard. Once this is done, everything will be fine. This would also help you deal with the slight chance that you have a nervous disorder, though it's not likely. If you take care of yourself, you can be sure to stay healthy for the whole month. Pay a little more attention to how well your teeth are doing.

Travel

The horoscope from the stars doesn't tell us anything beneficial about travel. Writers, poets, and people like them may not have the best trips. In fact, some of them could be seriously hurt by how unproductive their trips are.

You would travel alone mostly by train or car, but you would also take a fair amount of flights. A journey overseas is also not out of the question. But it's not likely that these efforts would lead to even a holiday, which might not be all that fun. The best direction to go is West.

Insight from the stars

You can say what you want; there's no problem with that. But don't forget to be nice if you don't want to make yourself more enemies. You are surrounded by the right kind of energy, which will help you have a positive outlook on life.

March 2023

Horoscope

The doors open, and barriers come down. The relationship problems get better. The energies that come from Pisces make these small miracles happen.

When Saturn moves into this sign on the 8th, it repairs the bonds that arguments and criticism have broken. You have more time for yourself and others because of all the good vibes. There are good things about being you. In your case, you feel more comfortable.

As time goes on, you have more room to move. After a hard time, you feel like you're starting over. Venus tries to get back together with someone or an old love starting on the 17th. If you still have doubts, Mars will show you how you really feel as early as March 26.

Love

This area that gives you trouble is taken care of by the energies that come from Pisces. They get rid of the differences by putting you in touch with people who have the same values as you. This month, the stars show you how much they love you. In exchange, don't look for bad things everywhere.

Slowly, exchanges based on mutual understanding are starting up again. Your relationship determines where it stands, what it excels at, and how it can assist you. From the 17th, agree to do what your partner wants for the sake of your relationship.

Single Scorpio, Over time, things fall into place so that you can have a good relationship with someone. Rather than leaving it on the doorstep, if you want it to last, make room for it in your life.

Career

Saturn's move into the sign of Pisces is like a soothing balm. You feel more comfortable putting your many skills to use. The sky is clear. You think no one can stop you from getting where you want. If someone gives you a surprise offer at the month's end, take it immediately. You won't be sorry, because it will help you make more money.

A month with lots of great chances to move up in your career. Like a hunter, you would work very hard and go after your goals with a single-minded focus. This would make sure that it works.

There is a good chance that your job will improve or that your business will have to make significant changes. Any change, though, should be made only after careful thought. This is even more important because you might feel a little bit scared even though things are going well for you.

Finance

On the financial side, this area doesn't cause any particular problems, but it would be nice if they could get better. So, if luck passes and it goes in your direction, do not ask yourself unanswerable questions.

However, the horoscope has nothing good to say about your financial future this month. There are signs that you will lose a lot of money when you trade stocks. So, you should stay away from any kind of risky business. Relationships with your bosses or coworkers are also likely to worsen to the point where a significant loss is almost inevitable.

But you can stop this from happening if you work hard and plan ahead. Some of you would also put too much effort into making money that can't be tracked. You should not do this, and it could get you into trouble. The climate would also make it hard to invest or start something new.

Health

The constellations that face you this month favor your health and well-being. Patients with a history of sensitive gastrointestinal tracts or other gastrointestinal disorders should expect great relief this month. Coughs, colds, and asthma, which are all common disorders of the chest, will be eliminated.

With good dental care, you can ensure that nothing bad occurs to your teeth. There is a reason to be concerned about the condition of your teeth. It's possible that you're easily agitated and have a little disturbed state of mind. You can keep your mental and physical health in excellent shape with extra care and exercise.

Travel

There isn't much chance of making money from travel this month, since the stars don't look good on this front. Most of the time this month, you would travel alone, mostly by car or train, with some air travel thrown in.

Also, you might work or travel abroad. But it is almost certain that these efforts would not bring the profits, pleasure, and satisfaction that were hoped for. The best direction would be to go West.

Insight from the stars

All the lights must be green for your deepest wishes to come true. If you say yes instead of no, this little miracle will happen. Make sure you do something worthwhile every day of your life. Don't waste your time and energy on things that won't help you get ahead.

April 2023

Horoscope

This month, some relationship problems are likely due to the fast-moving planets in Taurus. You can be stubborn about small things. From your point of view, you might seem suspicious for no good reason. But don't worry, nothing too bad is going to happen because Saturn and Mars are sending you their wise and kind energy.

You can't get on the wrong side of the force if you use these energies. Instead, they try to get you to look at things differently. They make you want to be kind, which brings smiles, trust, and mutual respect back. If it is too much, Saturn and Mars gently reframe what is most important. Because of this, fights don't last as long as they used to. They turn into something helpful and rewarding.

Love

This month, don't get into a fight, no matter how intense the urge is. Both you and the person you want to seduce should hold back. Take your time instead. Pay attention to the talks. Deepen the bonds. If you do these things, you'll be able to build a relationship based on real, long-lasting feelings.

Scorpio in a relationship, Saturn and Mars keep things on track, but Taurus' energies try to stir up trouble. Don't listen to words that bother you. Instead, be brave enough to show the tenderness you keep hidden for unknown reasons.

Single Scorpio, Your happiness lies with someone who isn't like the people you usually date. This month, learn to control your instincts and move slowly. This increases the likelihood of your wish coming true.

Career

As difficult as it may be, this industry is thriving. You may put your abilities to use for the second time this month as you have done so brilliantly. It's appreciated that you've taken the time to share your thoughts. Unfortunately, you may run against conservatives who are adamant about sticking to their guns when it comes to beliefs and practices. Your business will suffer if you engage in strife, Scorpio. On the other hand, saying yes to everything and acting on your instincts will have a greater impact.

Opportunities for progress in your job might arise from favorable situations. To achieve your goals, you would have to put in the effort. If this were to open up a whole new world of possibilities for you, you might end up with a better career or an entirely new company model. Fortunately, everything has turned out better than expected.

You should also plan on doing a lot of traveling since this will be quite useful. This time period will be marked by a willingness to take risks in your professional endeavors. This would lead to more efficient operations and better leadership skills.

Finance

Even though there is enough money to cover daily needs, a return of funds could be long overdue. Follow it so that the delays don't get too long.

The stars say that this month, things will go in your favor financially. In fact, there are clear signs that investing would bring you a lot of money. Because of this, it would be wise to start a new business or investment.

This month, you will win the big prize. Your business will do well, and you will put money into another business that needs your knowledge and skills in your field.

With so many ways to make money, it's no surprise that you'll be able to buy the things you need and want to make your life easier. Yes, you will have more money, and you can live well this month. But watch out for the people around you. You probably know how to handle your money well, but not how to deal with your feelings.

There are also signs that you will almost certainly come out on top if you get into a fight or go to court.

Health

This month, there's not much in the stars that's good news for your health. If you tend to get sudden, severe illnesses like fevers or inflammations, this could be a problem for you. You would need to pay more attention and get treatment immediately. This is something you must do quickly.

There is another reason to be aware of the chance of a bothersome eye infection that could cause problems. You must take the proper precautions to keep this from happening, like keeping things clean and taking the right medicine. The next few months won't be good for your health, so you should take even better care of yourself.

Travel

There's nothing particularly good about what the stars say about what you'll get out of travel. This month, you would travel on your own, mostly by car and train, with some flights.

A tour of another country is also possible. There's a good chance that all of these efforts won't lead to the profits or happiness that were hoped for. This is a pretty dark picture, but it is true. A lot of your travel may not be necessary, and you could get by just fine without it. The best way to go is to the East.

Insight from the stars

Despite what it seems like, conflicts are meant to shake up things that are stuck. This month, be open and willing to listen. You will be glad you did it. This month, your finances will improve because your investments will finally start to pay off.

May 2023

Horoscope

Since last month, relationship problems caused by Uranus and Mercury in Taurus have been a sign that something will change. It happens on the 17th when Jupiter moves into Taurus. The fact that the lucky star and evolution are in opposition to your sign means that your peace will be disturbed. How? By chances that come up out of nowhere but are silently hoped for.

This month, you can make changes, but they can't get in the way of your goals. Take the time to learn what is being asked of you if you want to do well in this little trick. Also, stay true to your habits by keeping your projects quiet. With Mars in Leo starting on the 21st, pay close attention to what shines instead of rejecting it.

Love

If you agree, your love can go to a new level. To do this, you will need to smile at luck instead of trying to get rid of it. Ignore outside influences if you want to pull off this little miracle. This will help you look deeper into situations or people.

Scorpio in a relationship, With Taurus's energy, it's not always easy to keep things in balance. The arrival of Jupiter can make things easier or harder. If you have something to say, do it nicely. This will stop the imbalance.

Single Scorpio, Everything looks good. You might meet someone, or a friendship might get stronger. Mars gives you a challenge starting on the 21st! If you agree to do it, your love will take the turn you wanted.

Career

The long-awaited progression is finally starting to look its best. But the choice is up to you. Scorpio, if you want, your current situation can get a lot better, but only if you're willing to work as a team. Take the time to think about it if it bothers you because you have it. Don't say "no" until the other person is done talking. Listen to the whole thing and ask for some time to think about it.

This is a good month to get ahead at work. Those who like art and those who work in the fine arts can look forward to a time when their creative work will be very satisfying. Some of you may even go on to make a name for yourselves with the things you do.

There is a chance that you would move where you do business or work, whether for a job or a business. But think carefully before making any changes since a hasty move could easily undo a lot of your hard work.

Finance

On the money side, be careful not to mix up cash receipts and expenses around the 5th. Be extra clear and make sure you know exactly where you are.

This month, the way the stars are lined up doesn't look good for your finances. First of all, there is a good chance that your relationships with your bosses will get worse, so much that it would become very likely that serious losses would happen. You need to think ahead and plan ahead to stop this from happening.

Spending a lot of money is always a red light. When managing your money, make sure you're making smart choices and that you've followed your plans for figuring out risks. If you invest in a company in distress, you might lose it.

You would almost certainly lose a lot of money if you made investments, so you shouldn't start any new businesses or trade stocks. There is also a chance that some of you might focus too much on making money that can't be tracked. Such activities wouldn't be good for you, so you should try to stay away from them.

Health

The way the stars are aligned for you this month makes it unlikely that your health will improve. Chronic diseases like rheumatism and digestive system problems like flatulence and too much diarrhea would cause you a lot of trouble, and you would have to pay much more attention to getting the proper medical treatment.

Also, you shouldn't let yourself get too irritable or nervous, and you shouldn't let your teeth get worse. This is a good month, and if you pay extra attention, you can make sure nothing bad happens. Overall, it is a month where you have to be careful.

Travel

The stars don't show that this is an excellent time to travel, so this is not a good month to go on a trip. Writers, poets, and people like them may have a stretch of financially and creatively unproductive travel.

You would usually travel alone, mostly by car or train, but you would also fly a fair amount. A trip to another country can't be ruled out. But it is almost certain that these efforts won't reach even a tiny part of the goals. The best way to go is to the South.

Insight from the stars

Jupiter and Mars bring movement back into your life in different ways. Instead of rejecting it, try to get it under control. You won't be sorry. It's never too late to make up with the people you care about. You need them in your life, so you should stop fighting and get along.

June 2023

Horoscope

Since last month, a change has started, and Jupiter is the symbol of it. The lucky star is linked to Saturn and gives you chances to improve your life in a way that makes you feel safe and secure. This might sound good, but since Uranus is still around, we should expect these changes to happen in fits and starts and not always smoothly.

This month, the opportunity that comes is represented by the Leo sign. It will be hard to negotiate, but you will get a nice improvement or win. You'll have to go against your nature for this little miracle to work. How? By telling people what they want to hear and putting their minds at ease about things that worry them.

Love

After a time of peace and quiet, your loves become filled with passion. Even though this sign makes you nervous, don't worry. Everything will be fine. Unless, for unknown reasons, you turn into a tyrant and oppressive version of yourself.

Scorpio in a relationship, When Venus and Mars are in Leo, fights and complaints take on a different tone. You have a choice this month. Either give them some room, and everything will be fine, or add fuel to the fire.

Single Scorpio, By chance, Venus brings you together with a lovely person. Even though this sign is not what you want, don't ignore this charming person. Instead, pay attention to them. You will be surprised by how good they are as people.

Career

You have the power to change your career. All you have to do is make the right choice. Scorpio, if you want to change things up, you'll have to deal with things that make you mad. So stay calm so you can finish the negotiations in your favor. After that, you can do whatever you want, because your skills are in demand.

In terms of your professional prospects, it is a good month. People who work in the fine arts and others like them would have a very good time. Some of you may even make a name for yourselves with what you bring to the table. There are signs that you are likely to work hard and go after your goals intelligently. And you will be able to do this.

There may even be a change in where your business or service is done. Though changing might be a good idea, you should only do so after careful thought. There would also be a lot of travel, which would be very helpful in the long run.

Finance

Your daily life is financially secure, and your piggy bank works like a charm. But don't be fooled by how you feel.

However, there's nothing particularly good about your financial prospects this month because the stars aren't in your favor. Clearly, taking risks in business would cause you to lose a lot of money. The lesson is clear: you shouldn't invest in stocks or do anything else that could go wrong.

Also, there is a chance that your relationships with your bosses will get so bad that losses become a real possibility. Take steps to fix the problem early on to stop this from happening. The environment wouldn't be great for making investments or starting new projects. Plans like these should be put on hold for now.

Health

The way the stars are aligned this month doesn't look good for your health. Overwork and weariness can lead to a general condition of weakness, with nervous disorders making matters even more difficult. If you don't want this to happen, don't put yourself under undue stress.

Another reason to be very careful about your dental health which could give you some trouble. Any bone injury should also be treated immediately since it could lead to trouble. In general, a pretty good month for your health.

Travel

This is a month when you should make a lot of money from travelling because the stars are aligned in a good way. All kinds of artists should find travel exciting and helpful for getting their creative juices flowing.

This month, you would most likely travel alone by car, train, and a fair amount by plane. A trip abroad is also a possibility. You would travel for business and other reasons, but no matter your goal, you would achieve it or just have a pleasant trip. The best direction to go is West.

Insight from the stars

To make the changes you want, you must take steps. This month's changes will require you to be at peace with what stands out by listening to your gut. Do not escape your responsibilities and obligations. Be someone who other people can count on.

July 2023

Horoscope

Again, the energies of Leo stop the evolution that Jupiter represents. Even so, the tensions calm down, and you find your clarity. Mars moves to Virgo on the 11th, and happiness never comes by itself. From that point on, you have all the power you need to negotiate the offers you get in a way that works for you.

Providence brings you together with people who can help you complete your projects. But you will still have to deal with the problems that come from Leo. Don't get too comfortable between the 12th and the 28th. Instead, watch everything and take the time to get the details right. Don't be afraid to say what you want.

Love

Venus in Leo is still making you feel the passion. Everything could go well, or they could fall into the destructive paths of desire. If you want peace, don't add fuel to the fire because you already know what will happen.

Scorpio in a relationship, The situation can be hard to handle until the 10th. Now that Mars is in Virgo, you can make sense of things. Your couple might have some fights until the end of the month, but you'll stick together.

Single Scorpio, You evolve in different worlds. So, you can expect to meet people who are attractive because of how they look and people who are attractive because of how smart they are. Listen to your intuition. She looks out for your best interests.

Career

Discords from Leo make it challenging to move forward. You like the opportunities that come your way, but they have problems that make you decide not to take them. Since problems never happen by themselves, you feel sad. You aren't very friendly, which isn't a good thing. Scorpio, if someone makes you an offer after the 11th, you should take it even if there are things about it that bother you. Why? Because in a few weeks, they will be gone.

This month, you will have good opportunities to advance in your career. This month will almost certainly be marked by hard work. You would be so focused on reaching the goals that you would put in everything you could to get the job done. This month, this will bring a lot of success.

There would be a lot of travel involved, which may or may not be advantageous in the long run. Aside from traveling, you would probably also change the place where you work or run your business. This would also be good for your future plans, which will happen this month. All in all, a really fruitful month.

Finance

Even though nothing bad is said about the economy, this area can worry you. Leave old problems behind.

The way the stars are aligned for you this month is anything but good for your finances. Some of you will almost certainly lose money if you speculate. So, avoiding all kinds of gambling would be a good idea.

There are also reasons to think that you might argue with your bosses so much that your relationship with them worsens, causing you to lose a lot of money. You can avoid this if you make an effort and can stop this from happening by taking the right steps ahead of time. This month, the climate is not good for making investments or starting new projects.

Health

The stars have not bestowed any health blessings on you this month. As a result, additional caution and attention are required. Those who are more likely to get piles should be very careful about what they eat and how they are treated. Carelessness would only make things worse.

Any tendency to get colds or have a lot of mucus come out may worsen. Again, this could need quick attention and corrective actions to make things right. Stones and a tendency to get fistula would also need more attention, as would your teeth. Take care of your teeth during this time since this could also cause you discomfort.

Travel

A month in which severe losses from travel are possible, as the stars are not very helpful in this regard. During your travels, you might get hurt or have some other kind of physical problem. Exercise care and minimize risks.

You would travel largely by road and train, with some air travel thrown in for good measure. A journey overseas is also not out of the question. These journeys could end up being utterly useless in every way. Since only some of them would be done for business purposes, they wouldn't make the expected money. The rest wouldn't make you happy. The North is the best direction.

Insight from the stars

Your success depends on how well you can combine discernment and persistence. After that, you won't be forced to make hard decisions. If you want great things to happen in your life, you need to take the first step.

August 2023

Horoscope

You are being pressured to accept a social or emotional commitment by Jupiter and Uranus. A marriage proposal or a request for professional cooperation can be made to you. Unfortunately, you likely disagree because of the dissonances brought on by Leo. On your darkest days, you consider these viewpoints to be a curse. You exhibit an attitude that shows lack of interest when you are more cheery.

Fortunately, Mars and Mercury in Virgo inspire you to consider offers made to you more thoroughly. Instead of concentrating on those who are less optimistic, they urge you to see the good side. If you don't want to lose an opportunity, go beyond your convictions this month.

Love

Venus is still in Leo and is also retrograde at the moment. Do not view a hesitancy or an accident as a sign of impending treachery if you want to avoid needless devastation that you will later regret. It will be more beneficial to maintain composure and remain impartial.

Scorpio, You must be accessible to your partner to spend time with them and listen to them if you want your relationship to be peaceful. Unfortunately, your relationship will experience unending turmoil if you are distracted.

Single Scorpio, You are placed in challenging circumstances by Venus' dissonances. Its backward motion accentuates this effect. You can choose for simplicity if you like. How? By paying close attention to those with whom you truly connect.

Career

The stars agree on everything this month! An offer of a partnership must be considered, and you must also accept it as a bonus. Because you have already experienced disappointments, Scorpio, do not place too much emphasis on particulars. Use this experience to your advantage instead. How, What, or Both? by resolving the minor issues and developing your abilities. Consider your passions while also finding your smile and business sense.

Given the favorable star alignment confronting you this month, you should have plenty of opportunities to

develop your job. Expect to travel frequently and for
the best of reasons.

You would typically put forth a lot of effort and
pursue your goals with businesslike efficiency. This
would do fantastically well. There is also a good
chance that the location of activities, such as a job or
business, may shift. This would also be a good thing.
Overall, this month would be quite helpful for your job
aspirations, and a lot may be accomplished during this
time.

Finance

If you take advantage of what is being presented to
you, this industry's financial performance will improve
much more.

A prosperous month in terms of your financial
potential. Many of you might anticipate enjoying a
bountiful crop of unexpected rewards. Many of you
might gain by speculating as well. Another possibility
is that an old friend may do you a favor that might
easily result in financial gain.

Additionally, you'll have a way of dealing with your
superiors this month that will make the relationship
very favorable for you. This may represent a
significant benefit. Lastly, forming relationships with
many intellectually and spiritually brilliant individuals

would be advantageous to you on both a monetary and
spiritual level.

Health

You should stay in excellent health for most of this
month because the stars are in a great mood to bless
your health. Any propensity for episodes of abrupt
acute illness, such as fevers and inflammation, would
be greatly reduced. They most likely wouldn't trouble
you at all.

People with any kind of dental issue will also be
affected by this. In fact, any problem with your
dentures should be taken carefully and has a strong
probability of being resolved. Your health is in good
hands right now, and those who are currently healthy
may anticipate maintaining that health.

Travel

This month's travel prospects just won't materialize,
and neither will the fun and pleasure that go along with
them since the stars aren't in your favor. Planning a
pilgrimage to a sacred location may be delayed, or
problems may arise while carrying it out. The
possibility that your dedication will carry you through
is something entirely else.

You would typically go alone by road or train with some air travel. Even a journey abroad is possible. However, none of these initiatives would be very fruitful. The best direction is east.

Insight from the stars

Be more open to those you love and pay close attention to what others say. You will avoid the inconvenience, which lowers your mood. Most areas of your life will see good fortune. Because of work well done, you should be proud of yourself.

September 2023

Horoscope

You profit from the influence of those who can help you evolve a part of your life thanks to the favorable effects of planets in friendly signs.

You get proposals, and opportunities come up. People are willing to talk with you, and your expertise and background are in high demand, so you might be curious about the issue in this specific advantageous circumstance. You and your convictions, which drive you only to see the negative in opportunities that come your way, are its physical manifestation.

If you agree, do not use the failures of the past as a guide this month since they will only encourage you to reject everything in its entirety. Consider them learning experiences that you can put to good use.

Love

Venus' dissonances cause conflict and uncertainty in your romantic relationships. Your feelings are strong, and suddenly, your relationships are challenging. If you don't want to be alone, consider your options carefully or take a step back.

Venus ignites the fire in your relationship, while Mercury prompts thoughtful and fruitful conversations. By being open and honest this month, you can reduce tension. Avoid talking about specifics of the past, though; it won't be helpful.

Single Scorpio, A wonderful encounter creates distance and closeness with a known person. You may choose between complexity and simplicity this month. So give it some thought before making a choice.

Career

This industry is a delicate topic this month. You examine what is being provided to you with suspicion. On your worse days, you come across as disinterested. Scorpio, don't turn down an offer. Still, have a look. Don't concentrate on the negative. Be optimistic and consider all the options available to you. Avoid alienating those who appear to be excessively superficial while you're doing it.

In the upcoming month, intriguing opportunities for work progress ought to materialize. Your working style would help you succeed. You have a businesslike efficiency and are action-oriented. You would typically put in a lot of effort and receive a lot of credit for it.

Encouraged by your success, you could decide to expand by changing your operation's location, whether a job or a business. All of this would be done to improve your chances of success. Look forward to making a huge accomplishment this month.

Finance

The necessities of daily existence are taken care of in terms of money. However, your leisure money is drastically decreased unless you make the appropriate business choice.

This month's financial outlook is quite promising, and it might put you on a firm financial foundation for the long term. You may enjoy a bountiful crop of unexpected benefits and would profit through speculation, which would result in significant gains.

You already have a style of managing your subordinates or workers to get the most out of them. You'd gain a lot from this, which may lead to a lot of money. In addition, an old buddy may be willing to help you out in some way, which would be a huge help. Finally, your relationships with your superiors will take on such pleasant dimensions that you will gain greatly from them.

Health

Since Lady Luck is in the mood to bless your health, you can expect to stay healthy during this time. People with chronic illnesses like rheumatism and similar problems like flatulence and too much gas in the digestive tract can expect to feel better if they normally take care of themselves. This is also true for any tooth pain.

Also, if you tend to be nervous, you can expect that to go away and cause much less trouble than usual. You might feel physically weak, but this is easy to fix with some exercise and good food. A good month in which you probably won't face any serious health problems.

Travel

A month when it doesn't look like you'll make much money from traveling because the stars aren't in a good mood. You would probably travel by train, car, and air a fair amount when you were by yourself. Also, a trip abroad is not out of the question.

All these trips might be related to work and other things equally. But no matter why you're doing these things, it's almost certain that you won't reach even a fraction of your goals. As a result, it's a good idea to go over your travel plans ahead of time to see if they'll get you anywhere. The best direction to go would be East.

Insight from the stars

You're well aware that crises don't end well. So consider and evaluate the circumstances and happenings. By doing this, you will get success right away. Your home environment will be one of harmony and calm.

October 2023

Horoscope

Your growth is going as planned. The planets that develop in Virgo support it. Despite these thoughtful preparations, you struggle to make a choice. On your worst days, you strongly dislike what is given to you. By discouraging past events, you are motivated to accomplish nothing more until the 12th.

On March 13, Mars enters your sign. It motivates you to take action and make choices. Act calmly and wisely if you want your expansion to be long-lasting. Spend some time reflecting while your head is resting. If you must, wait until the 23rd. Why? Because when Mercury enters your sign, it will sharpen your insight and intuition. You'll have the ability to choose wisely.

Love

When Venus moves into Virgo on the 10th, your loves find peace that makes you want to give your best. Beautiful things make you feel good and happy. It's fun. But bad memories make it hard to bring up your feelings. You find your mind at the end of the month.

Problems from the past have a terrible habit of returning to the surface. Change the subject if you want peace! Also, show your partner that you care about them. Do things that make you happy. By doing this, you will bring harmony back to your relationship.

Single Scorpio, Mars, and Venus bring you together with someone you already know. Don't force anything if you have trouble investing. You should be more at ease by the end of the month.

Career

You have had time to consider what has been suggested since last month. You get to make a choice this month since Mars enters your sign on the 13th. Scorpio, the decision is yours! You may either harness this energy for your benefit or use it against you. Therefore, now is the moment to combine your intuition with your experience if you truly want things to proceed in the correct direction. You'll end up with this tale that overwhelms you if you do this.

A month full of intriguing chances for job progress as the stars seem to be on your side. To achieve your goals, which you will pursue with businesslike efficiency, you tend to work extremely hard. You could change the location of operations during this phase, whether it be a job or a business. All of this would be for the best.

In addition, there would be a lot of traveling. You may feel a bit uneasy, which might bother you a little. In fact, there's a potential that some of you would be tempted to break the law to make quick money. Such tendencies should be stopped firmly.

Finance

Financially, although the end of the month is assured, leisure time is constrained until you decide to alter the situation.

A highly beneficial month in terms of your financial possibilities. You would benefit greatly from any unexpected earnings and profit from the speculation, reaping significant gains.

You would be able to quickly and effectively benefit from your efforts. Others among you would know how to treat your juniors or subordinates in a way that would allow you to get the most value out of their assistance. This may very well be the most significant gain in a month that is otherwise highly profitable. Furthermore, there is a good chance that an old friend may do you a favor or earn you a sizable profit.

Health

This month, the stars in your direction have a lot of good news for your health. You can expect any tendency toward tooth trouble of one kind or another will improve. There is, however, a note of warning against overwork, as this could easily ruin a good situation. Make a new plan that doesn't put too much stress on your body.

If you ignore this, it could be terrible for your health. Everything else is fine. Having a tendency to be nervous wouldn't bother people who are already like this. As a rule, this is a relatively healthy month in which you are unlikely to encounter any significant health issues.

You probably won't face any serious health risks in a pretty good month.

Travel

There's nothing auspicious about what the stars say about what you'll get out of travel. This month, about half of your trips would be for work or business, and the other half would be for other reasons.

You would probably travel alone most of the time, mostly by car and train. A trip abroad is also not impossible. No matter why or how you travel, you likely won't get even a fraction of what you planned to get out of it. Thinking carefully about your travel plans

before you make them would be wise. The best
direction to go would be West.

Insight from the stars

Don't make a bad decision because you think the
past has tricked you. Wait, and if you need to, take a
step back to adjust better how you react. This month,
you should pay close attention to your overall health.
To be useful, you need to be in good health.

November 2023

Horoscope

You can remain objective due to the planets in Virgo. Unfortunately, Venus departs you on the 8th, leaving you alone with Mars, Mercury, and the Sun in Scorpio.

The opposition between Jupiter and Uranus indicates that things will be tricky. Your argument will be illogical. Authoritarianism will result from your innate authority.

Unless you have the foresight to communicate with Saturn in Pisces, things will be different in these circumstances. You will pause to reflect. You will act with the efficiency that you are known for. Your natural skills will be shown to their maximum extent. The expansion of your position is subjugated to your inner understanding this month since it is your finest guide.

Love

Venus in Virgo will keep your affections alive till the 8th. His absence leaves you with these internal torments that drive you to withdraw. This, however, is avoidable. How? By recalling the pleasant moments, you shared with previous romances.

Scorpio, Everything in your relationship should be nice. To accomplish this tiny miracle, you must break your poor habit of sabotaging anything pleasurable. Take a step back this month before making a choice.

Scorpio single, Someone responsible and steady represents your happiness. You might be able to meet them this month. To do this, agree to go out of your sanctuary and, more significantly, pursue those negative memories that want to arise.

Career

You have two options this month. Either you react immediately and make a decision that will ruin your accomplishments, or you take a step back and everything will be alright. Don't take things literally, Scorpio! Take a step back and reflect. You will discover that everything is alright and that you have no need to be sad.

A favorable month in which you can significantly improve your career prospects. You are likely to work hard to achieve your goals. You would be quite successful at this. There would also be a lot of traveling, which would be advantageous.

Indeed, if you are encouraged by your success, there is a good likelihood that you will change the location of your operation, whether it is a job or a business. All of this would be for the better, but you should consider it carefully before making any changes.

Finance

On the financial front, while current expenses are guaranteed, your leisure budget is always kept to a bare minimum. However, as far as the stars are concerned, this is not a good month for your financial prospects. There is a significant risk that your relationships with your superiors may deteriorate to the point where you will have to incur a loss as a result. As a result, you must prepare for such a scenario and take preventive measures well in advance.

Possibilities would be scarce, and most of you would struggle to achieve your goals. There is also the risk that some of you may get overly focused on generating undeclared money. This will almost certainly have a negative impact on your whole position. Please correct this. Investments should be avoided as well.

Health

The stars are not in a good mood this month and will withhold their favor for your excellent health. Those prone to chilly hands and feet would have a difficult time. Any predisposition toward anxiety would be exacerbated. A skilled yoga instructor and consistent practice might do wonders for your ailment, allowing you to be free of your worries.

There is also the possibility that you will experience troubles as a result of tooth decay. This entails paying additional attention to and caring for your dental health. The period ahead is not good for your health and will need more attention and care.

Travel

A good month for reaping a bountiful crop of travel benefits, as the stars' omens are particularly favorable. Some of you would go on pilgrimages to holy locations, which would be a defining moment in your lives.

Those wishing to pursue further education or training in another country or location would have their plans carried out effortlessly. Business travel would be a huge success. You would largely travel by rail or road, with some air travel thrown in for good measure.

A trip overseas is also an option. The most favorable direction is North.

Insight from the stars

Your love life and business success are dependent on your wisdom. So, reject outside forces and take a step back. You will make the finest decisions this way. Your social life will improve because you are ready to step outside your comfort zone and meet new people.

December 2023

Horoscope

Venus is in your sign from the 5th to the 29th. This might make you seem hard to deal with, but things will be different this time.

From 2nd to 23rd, Mercury in Capricorn calms you down. Your feelings and thoughts are smooth because of these long-range and quiet waves.

Starting on the 14th, when you downgrade, you go backward. So, it's time to make peace with what couldn't be made peace with before. Mercury can help you change the way you think. It helps you realize that things will happen in the future. It shows you that you don't have to ruin everything to move on in life. Use this state of grace to incorporate your environment into your growth.

Love

Your romantic relationships will resume after a dry spell. The tribulations of the past disappear. You're ready to start loving again. You feel open to

experiencing new emotions. Mercury, who makes you
a pleasant person with other people, attests to this
minor miracle.

Mercury, which is linked to Venus, starts
conversations that aim to lay out your cards and talk
about your shared future. Take the chance to tell your
partner how you feel. This will clear up any questions
they have.

Single Scorpio, your sex appeal increases when
Venus is in your sign. You will have a lot of luck! For
the next step, you decide whether you can live a perfect
life or make a lifelong commitment.

Career

Wait till the fifth if you aren't sure what you want.
From this day forward, Venus begins to enlighten you.
It gives you instructions. Happiness is not a one-person
show. Mercury directs your attention to what matters
most. Scorpio, your business is about to embark on a
long-anticipated growth. Instead of wasting time
pondering these concerns, take advantage of this
current moment.

You will receive accomplishment awards for your
hard work, indicating that you are successful, credible,
and dependable in your profession. Regardless of your
work achievements, you should always be confident in
your abilities and strive to improve yourself.

Office rivalry will bring out the best in each of you. So, try hammering out new ideas and muster the guts to submit them to your superiors. If you are fortunate, you will win.

You'd have to put in a lot of effort to see results, but it would be worth it in the end.

Finance

On the money side, this area is favored, so you will have a lot of room to move. So make the appropriate choice, and you won't be in a panic at the end of the month.

Your progress at work will assist you in meeting your financial commitments. This indicates that you will not have a financial problem. However, you must be honest about your profits and spending. By monitoring your money, you will be able to determine if you will be able to meet your responsibilities on time or whether you will need to seek a loan to meet your obligations.

Health

This month, the Gods are on your side regarding your health. You won't have serious health problems this month if you're lucky. Any tendency to get sick quickly, like a fever or inflammation, would disappear, and these problems wouldn't bother you as much. Since this is a good month, such relief can be expected.

But there are reasons to be careful about your teeth. If you don't do this with care, it could hurt your teeth. You should also be careful if you break a bone, which is very unlikely during this month.

Travel

This isn't a good month for travel since the stars aren't aligned in a way that would make it a good idea. There is a chance that you will get hurt or have some other kind of physical problem while you are traveling. So, you should be careful and take the fewest possible risks.

Most of the time, you would travel by rail or road, but you would also fly a fair amount. Some of your trips might be related to your job or business. A good number of them wouldn't be so similar. It's pretty clear that none of these would be beneficial. A trip abroad is also not impossible. The best way to go is to the East.

Insight from the stars

It's safe to say that everything is in order for your expansion to go off as planned. Do not succumb to the temptation to take the short way; rather, follow the road of knowledge if you do. In order to appreciate your accomplishments, you must take the time to do so. Also, work on your deficiencies so they don't get in the way of your development.

Printed in Great Britain
by Amazon